Growing Up During
the
GREAT DEPRESSION

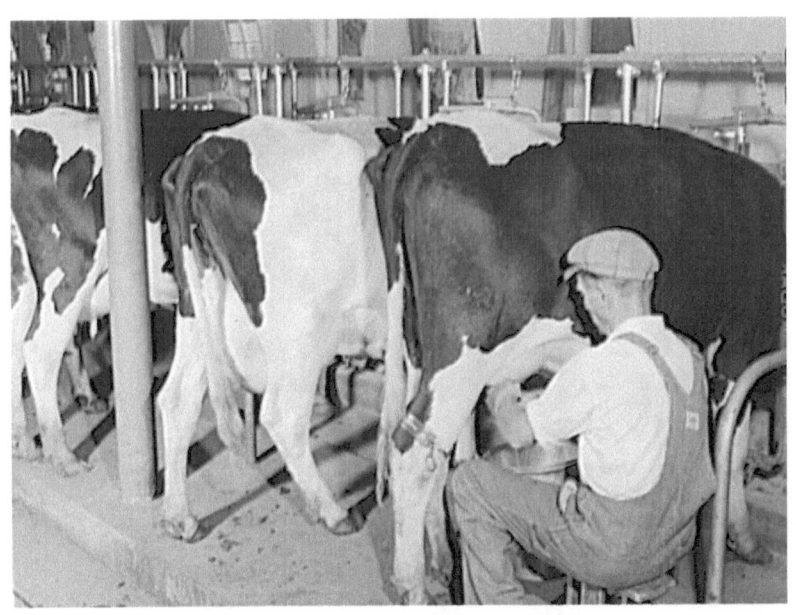

Library of Congress FSA/OWI LC-USF34-059455-D

CHARLES HUHTANEN

Order this book online at www.trafford.com
or email orders@trafford.com

Most Trafford titles are also available at major online book retailers.

Cover photo from Library of Congress Farm Security Administration/Office of War Information
(FSA/OWI) LC-DIG-fsac-1a34567 Farmland in the Catskill country, in New York State.

Printed in the United States of America.

ISBN: 978-1-4669-5168-6 (sc)
ISBN: 978-1-4669-5167-9 (e)

Trafford rev. 09/12/2012

 www.trafford.com

North America & International
toll-free: 1 888 232 4444 (USA & Canada)
phone: 250 383 6864 ♦ fax: 812 355 4082

Table of Contents

Foreword

Charles "Chuck" Huhtanen grew up during hard times in a hard place. Cheerfully living the only life he knew, he learned to enjoy that life, to make the most of what he had, and to better his condition and conditions. Hardly "the short and simple annals of the poor"* Chuck describes how his immigrant family survived adversity during The Great Depression while toiling on a hardscrabble farm in Upstate New York.

Imagine today living without a phone, TV, or even electricity, central heating, indoor plumbing, or running water. Then imagine growing your family's food . . . . or starving. Would you have your kids doing hard physical work at an early age? That is the life Chuck was born into, lived, and writes about with pleasant memories which will make you smile.

Read how a perspective can define conditions, and perhaps appreciate what, in spite of the present recession and your present troubles you can adapt, adopt, and, like Chuck win, despite . . . or because of . . . hard times and bad breaks. This is not just a story of survival. Read it carefully. It is a narrative of a mind-set which breezily can teach you how to survive and enjoy survival.

David Mack

* Thomas Grey's Elegy Written in a Country Churchyard

Prologue

O ur economy teeters on the brink of depression and circumstances are very different from those of the earlier Great Depression when many people lived on farms and were able to grow much of their food; now we have a vibrant, world-wide, computer driven economy; no longer can we depend on our own resources for sustenance but are largely dependent on huge agro-business companies. Life was simpler then but troubles were just as real.

Daniel D. Tompkins was the governor of New York State from 1807 to 1817; then he was elected the 6th Vice-President of the U.S. serving under James Monroe from 1817 to 1826. The county named for him was originally part of a much larger Albany County that was later split into a number of counties including Tompkins of 492 square miles with a population in 2010 of 101,564. Ironically Dan Tompkins never visited the county named after him.

During the Ice Age, glaciers covered nearly all of New York State; the latest about 21,000 years ago. They were the primary sculptors of Tompkins County where they left behind terminal moraines consisting mostly of rocks, and drumlins seen all over the state. Subsequent global warming created rivers that eroded the ice age sculptures and created the many gorges and waterfalls around Ithaca, the county seat. The glacial recession, although creating the beautiful Finger Lakes, also pushed most of the good farmable soil as far south as Lancaster County, Pennsylvania leaving behind many swamps and barely tillable soil.

The Huhtanen Farm

aymond Orteig, a wealthy New York restauranteur, offered a $25000 prize in 1919 to the first person to fly solo across the Atlantic; this was finally completed on May 21, 1927 by Charles Lindbergh. Two months earlier (March 30) in the same year in Ithaca, New York, Charles Norman Huhtanen entered the world; named perhaps after the famous aviator.

I never met my Grandfather Elias Huhtanen, he died the year before I was born, he emigrated from Finland around the turn of the century; probably entering the United States to Minnesota through the long unmanned border with Canada. He found work in an iron mine and after some years sent for his son George Elias Huhtanen (my father) who also came through Canada. My father at the time (1906) was about 12 years of age. He worked in iron mines in Minnesota and later worked as a lumberjack in Michigan where he married my mother, Ada Maria Muje; who had also emigrated from Finland. They subsequently moved to the town of Dryden in Tompkins County, New York, where a small Finnish community had planted roots; there they purchased a 72 acre farm about 5 miles from Ithaca. The land, overrun by the last glacier, was very poorly drained, rocky and unproductive but they set about making a go of it with the help of my oldest brother Wilho (Bill), a teenager at the time.

The farm was in very low land (much of it was indeed swamp) and it often flooded in heavy rains. I always marveled at the tremendous efforts of previous owners, who had cleared the land; some of it perhaps by my father. Along one edge of a large field were the remnants of very large tree roots that had been removed from the originally forested land and were used as fences. Another great feat was the draining of a large field with tiles that kept most of it dry enough to plow and seed; it was this field that once served as an airplane landing strip. The previous owner of our farm was the Van Tine family who moved to another tract (with less flooding) bordering the Eight Square School. The family was very progressive, they had installed a belt driven cooling apparatus in their milkhouse; they also had a large wall mounted telephone. The mother had tried to start a 4-H Club that I attended once. Ralph Van Tine Sr. also was the only one around who plowed his land with three horses. I often wondered if he or some previous farmers had needed sturdier oxen for land clearing.

The farm was purchased through a land bank in the northeast, perhaps Massachusetts. It was finally paid off many years later through my mother's efforts selling butter and eggs after trudging the 5 miles to Ithaca. The farm had two barns; one for the horses with a loft for storing hay and a chute for dropping the hay to the horses stabled below, often we had fun jumping onto the hay in the chute. The other barn was for cows with loft facilities for storing hay and equipment. Other buildings were an outhouse about 50 feet from the house, and a sauna, about 15 feet from the outhouse. Crops harvested were hay, corn, oats, buckwheat and garden vegetables, mainly potatoes. We could not afford tractors, the plowing and harrowing was done with horses. One memorable day, Bill was plowing a field with the horses, I, age 3 or 4, was following in the newly turned furrows. I was fascinated by the killdeers that dove into the newly turned earth seeking edible insects. Our automobiles of the 1920's were an open Star, a Franklin, and later, a versatile 1928 Chevrolet sedan that served as transportation but also was invaluable for bringing wood from the nearby forest.

Cutting wood for the stoves

I remember well the woodcutting forays in the winter months. Father always selected beech trees, they were easy to cut down and easy to split into stove length. One time the chosen tree was home to a honey bee hive and for some time we had delicious honey for added carbohydrate. The tree cutting process consisted first in chopping a V-shaped guide about two feet high, then finishing the job with a two man crosscut saw on the opposite side; as a young kid of 8 or 9, I tried to master this instrument which required close cooperation with the partner to maintain the proper downward pressure at the correct time, otherwise one person would end up doing the whole job. My father did not succeed in making a good woodsman of me.

Many years later I thought that I was qualified to cut down a tree for a friend, it was too close to the house. It was a cool, windy day. I cut the notch on the side of the tree opposite the house with an axe, then we used a chain saw, starting correctly from the side near the house to complete the task. Nearing the end of the sawing I realized that the wind was blowing hard from the side of the V cut and was binding the saw, this meant that the tree would fall toward the house! We quickly put a wedge in the saw cut and scurried around to find rope enough to tie to the tree and to my friend's Toyota. After some anxious moments the Toyota pulled the tree safely away from the house!

The younger boys had the job of sawing branches with a bucksaw while father and the older boys sawed the fallen tree into manageable blocks. The wood was loaded in the back of the Chevy. With the seats removed and chains in place, father drove the car home through the snow about a quarter mile away. There the logs were split into smaller pieces with some help from the boys, me included. I remember when I was trying to master the splitting process with an axe, my efforts were too inefficient for my father who got mad and knocked me down with his fist. He knocked me down another time when we were on the road to Ithaca for some reason that I do not remember; it was in the winter and was snowing when we had a flat tire. Father fixed the tire and then had an altercation with mother, I intervened trying to protect mother when he hit me with his fist. I probably had it coming being of a mulish (father's description) disposition! But I nevertheless respected my father for his manifold abilities in carpentry, auto mechanics, as a cobbler repairing our shoes and in many other recession mandated tasks.

LC-USF33-011063-M4

Early pre-school years

I was the youngest of the four boys; Bill was the oldest born in 1918, then Carl, George (Evert) and me. Evert was 18 months older than I, Carl was 5 years older. Carl was always a special brother; when I was 14 he gave me his prized bicycle; he had earned enough money from helping local farmers to buy a new car. This bicycle was my pride and joy. Previously I had had to resort to scavenging the Ithaca dump for parts to build my own bicycle; it ended up without tires or wheel bearings but it was nevertheless a treasured accomplishment. Trips to the dump through neighbor's fields were frequent for us kids; I found there my first belt and wore it for many years as a memento of those lean times until my wife, without informing me, discarded it. I once brought home an electric clock and could never understand why it did not work when I connected it to my father's car battery! One time in the late fall we went to the Cornell University dump and came away with discarded shoulder pads from the football team, but we could not find any use for them.

Some very poignant memories of my early childhood remain with me even to this year of 2012. Once our parents piled all of us kids into the car and drove 30 miles to Auburn Amusement Park; what I remember most was the two flat tires on the way; these were expeditiously fixed by father.

Gasoline rationing was carefully monitored during the war by the Office of Price Administration (OPA); the A sticker for most cars allowed the purchase of four gallons a week for non-essential, non-pleasure use; workers essential to the war effort were given the green B stickers allowing the purchase of eight gallons per week; the off-road needs of farmers were

LC-USF34- 073807-D

met with the red R stickers. Many other items were also strictly rationed including rubber tires, women's nylons and aluminum metal.

Civilian Conservation Corps

resident Franklin Roosevelt introduced many helpful programs to aid the poor, one was the Civilian Conservation Corp that sent Carl to a work camp about 12 miles away. Our father drove us there once to collect Carl's salary that was designed to help with family expenses. On the way home father treated us to an ice cream cone (I think they cost 5 cents); this was the first time I had ever tasted ice cream!

Exploring the forests

y older siblings were in the local one room school for some years leaving me at home with two younger sisters; during those years I had a great time exploring the many nearby forests, a particular thrill was finding the nest of a marsh hawk in the swamp with eggs in it. The mother hawk dove at me and screeched in the hawk fashion to drive me away. I played with woodchucks, standing over their hole after seeing them go in. With a nailed stick in hand I stood quietly over their hole for hours expecting to clobber them when they came out but I later discovered that the wily chuck always made a second escape hole without the characteristic mound of excavated dirt at the exit! Once I found mosquito larvae thriving in the sap or water of a hole in a tree. Later when I was in 4th or fifth grade, the teacher was telling us about fossils, I knew from my explorations where a rock with a fossilized trilobite was. She was excited when I brought it in and showed it to the students.

The old swimming hole

Though it was the depression we kids were not unhappy; we played, we roamed the forests, we had Fall Creek just a mile away where we often went with our buddies to fish for suckers or to swim. We looked forward to the end of May when we were finally allowed to go barefoot, which was when the tree leaves were the size of a hand. We learned to swim by jumping in and getting out as best we could. One time we tried to teach a younger pal to swim; but he could not manage it and went under water; we pulled him out and managed to get the water out of his lungs, but it was a close call. At first we used water wings of cloth blown up with several breaths of air; these went flat quite quickly so we had no alternative but to swim on our own. We had sling shots made of tree branches with a piece of a discarded inner tube for the sling, we pelted birds with small stones but seldom succeeded in hitting any of them. Once we pelted a white-faced hornets nest with our sling shots and made a rapid retreat when they lit out after us; with great care and rapid footsteps we escaped unstung.

Airplane

An exciting thrill occurred one day around 1934 when an airplane landed in a nearby bumpy field. The pilot was Bob Conlon, husband of Jennie, my father's half-sister; they lived nearby in East Lansing. He gave rides to the neighbors but the kids were not invited. Some years later just before the start of WWII, we watched in awe while pilots flying out of the Ithaca airport in Fairchild trainers practiced touchdowns in a neighbor's field. I was stuck on flying; in later years I had a plane of my own, an Ercoupe, a low wing, underpowered but beautiful machine.

Pre-teen years

Above all . . . we were ignorant of other peoples troubles; to us in our insular Finnish community our way of life was OK even though most homes (ours included) had no electricity, phones, or running water. During the depression we had only very basic foods to eat; mother gave us (ugh!) cod liver oil for Vitamin D; my older brother developed scurvy and was given oranges by the local welfare agency. We were on relief for much of the depression. I always admired a pal whose father had a steady job; he had rigged a gas powered generator in his garage that provided enough electricity for a few light bulbs. But for most of us (until the end of the war when Rural Electrification came) kerosene lamps and lanterns provided light. Water for drinking and cooking was from a bucket filled from a well about 75 feet from the house, this regularly froze on winter mornings when the temperature would often be 25 degrees below zero. Water for washing faces was from rain water caught and stored in a cistern in the cellar, a hand pump drew water into the kitchen.

With 8 children of all ages, sleeping arrangements were necessarily quite quixotic, when I was very young, about three, I remember sleeping in a bed with my mother and 2 or three siblings, my place was crosswise at the foot of the bed! Later I shared a room upstairs with Evert where, in the winter, snow would often filter through the only window. We always enjoyed the warm company of our cat. The only heat in the entire 7 room wooden frame, unpainted house was a stove in the front room fed with the wood we had gathered from the forest. Our upstairs bedroom was heated by the chimney of the stove that passed through the room. The chimney passed through a metal grate that had holes around it; one day coming home on the bus a girl handed me a note; I was so embarrassed that I hid the note in one of the holes! There it stayed and eventually burned but it may have easily caused a fire.

Our eating arrangements were informal, no fuss; meals were plebeian, just plain meat and potatoes, home made bread, milk and butter from our cows. We sometimes enjoyed apple or huckleberry pie or stale old welfare rolls. Breakfast was usually eggs, Shredded Wheat Muffets, Wheatena or oatmeal, but no coffee for youngsters. We were given Postum instead of coffee. Once we had a barrel of salted fish (probably herring) that lasted a long time, dried apricots were a common snack. School lunches were always thick homemade bread with peanut butter and jelly. We did not celebrate holidays, since our Finnish parents had not been assimilated into American culture.

I had three older brothers, we got on famously, I always had their old radios to play with (not working), a bicycle from Carl (it was like new and the joy of my life), their no longer used traps to catch animals for their pelts (I only caught one sellable weasel, story in another part of this dissertation), and of course their cast-off clothes including shoes. Father was also a good cobbler and many times re-soled the hand-me-down shoes and mother repaired sweaters and clothes. In fact I never had a new anything until later when I was a hired hand working on farms. So the products of the old spinning wheel, no longer in use but stored away for kids to play with, kept me in woolen stockings and sweaters for years. Mother had made them some time ago and still carefully darned them when holes developed.

LC-USF34-031625-D

The fire

here was a real fire at our farm, a devastating fire in the middle of that great depression; it changed forever the hopes and aspirations of our parents. I was one of the arsonists; the other was my older brother Evert. This happened probably around 1932 or 1933. My older brothers had been setting off fireworks during the fourth of July celebrations but Evert and I were too young to be allowed to handle firecrackers and we had no way to get them since we had no money and no way to get to the dealer 5 miles away. One day we got hold of some "punk", a long burning stick material used by our older brothers for setting off firecrackers. We hid in the barn and experimented with lighting the punk and other small wooden sticks. After a while we were through experimenting and left the barn. About 1 or 2 hours later the barn started to burn; I was hustled off to a neighbor and vividly remember watching the barn burn to the ground. I realized that we had not taken care to extinguish the burning sticks before leaving, thinking that the smoldering sticks would go out by themselves. At our ages of 5 or 6 we had no idea of the dangers associated with playing with fire. I have never discussed the barn fire with anyone but the memory now is as vivid as on that fateful day watching it from the neighbor's steps.

That fire completely changed our family. I was too young to understand the implications of losing our livelihood in the midst of the great depression. We were never associated with the fire and if there were suspicions no mention of our involvement was ever made. My father and a neighbor set up a saw mill and made a bunch of boards intending to re-build the barn (the horse barn was saved) but the lumber lay outside for a number of years before eventually rotting. Instead of rebuilding, a formidable task, Father at first made a little money on odd jobs as a carpenter and by sharpening neighbors saws but later he became such a good carpenter that he was chosen to build a house for a friend.

With help he poured the foundation, then he lived there eating mostly cheese sandwiches until it was finished some months later. I visited him once riding the bicycle that my brother had given me. I was proud of his handiwork.

The sauna

An indispensable feature of Finnish communities was the weekly sauna. The wood frame building had a 50 gallon oil drum filled with rocks and with a fire pit underneath. The rocks were heated for most of the day before it was ready. Entry was through an anteroom used for dressing. The inside had two tiers of benches; the top one was for the diehards, because it was the hottest. Water was splashed onto the hot rocks and hot air and steam filled the room, for added effect a tree switch applied to the body could be used to enhance the self-inflicted torture. Cold water and scrubbing ended the procedure, after which we ran back to the house, often through snow. Most of the time the unused sauna was a favorite habitat of a variety of snakes, usually the harmless garter or milk snake.

Growing our food

The vegetable garden was extremely important during the depression. We also supplemented it by picking high bush huckleberries from a swamp. One day the whole family went on a huckleberry picking expedition and had a picnic lunch. We kids ate most of what we picked but father and mother each picked a good sized pailfull. The huckleberries made delicious pies but they were also canned for winter. Potatoes were stored in the cellar. Once apples were also stored in the cellar but they rotted and were useless. A few times apples were dried by hanging slices in the living room for several months.

Mother was a very practical cook, using the limited available resources to greatest advantage. I remember the Finnish style bread she made for our sandwiches at school. I envied the "store boughten" bread other kids had for lunches while we had coarse "home made". She would make pies quite often, mostly from apples or huckleberries. Our farm had once been owned by fruit lovers, there were a number of apple tree varieties surrounding the house, among them were Hendryx Sweet, Northern Spy, Baldwins, Greenings and several other varieties, some were best eaten off the tree, while others, especially the Northern Spy made excellent pies. In addition there were pear, butternut, chokecherry, hickory trees, gooseberry and large grape bushes. We could not wait for the fruit to reach maturity; often we kids would get fruit from neighbors' trees sans permission! Once I fell out of a tree and was unconscious for a while. Occasionally father would bring home day-old sweet rolls or dried apricots, probably from a government food bank. We often picked delicious wild strawberries from neighboring fields when they ripened in late June. Their taste remains vivid in my taste buds. Tree-ripened peaches were another taste sensation no longer available in modern grocery stores. Shipping requirements today trump consumer preferences.

A vegetable garden was mandatory; mostly it consisted of staples such as potatoes and beans that could be stored for long periods. Fields were planted with corn, oats or buckwheat.

Starting school

We kids spoke only Finnish at home until we mimicked the English our older siblings had picked up at school. After entering school I no longer wanted to speak Finnish and never spoke it again if I could help it. School for me started when I was 7 ½ years old having been born in March of 1927. My older sister taught me some English words and I remember how proud I was to be able to spell "electricity" even before entering the Eight Square Brick School on Henshaw Road.

Some modern historians call it the "Eight Square School" but to all of us students and parents, it was always the Eight Square <u>Brick</u> School. My theory is that the brick school built in 1826 replaced the former wooden school (also octagonal) that burned down; thus the spelling distinction. In a picture of our school taken in 1936, there were 17 students, one teacher and one dog sitting next to my brother. All of my siblings went to this school which was finally vacated around 1944; it became and still stands; a unique and authentic state historic site, a relic of early education in our town of Dryden in Tompkins County, NY. Today local school children with their teachers come to the school to imitate the students of several hundred years ago.

The Eight Square Brick School was about a mile from our home and we always had to walk to it, even in the snows and blizzards of mid New York State; there was no way of knowing if the teacher would show up; we had no telephones or radios. Actually I remember once going to school during a blizzard (dragging a sled!) only to trudge back home again through deepening snowdrifts when the teacher never showed up. The teachers were very conscientious, though, and cared deeply for their pupils. On my very first day in school I went home after not understanding her command announcing morning recess "you can go now"! My older brother was sent to get me and I had to walk back alongside him on his bicycle. The sympathetic teacher (Mrs. Freese from Freeville) sat with me, probably hugged me, and explained very tenderly to a crying miscreant how recess works. What an auspicious beginning to an education!

Reading material was provided by a roaming van "Library" where the students could borrow books for a month or more; for me the Burgess Animal books were always a pleasure to read. Interestingly the original Burgess Animal stories are still available in the Amazon store. We had a small collection of other books in the school including an encyclopedia and a dictionary, I remember reading of the exploits of Little Black Sambo, banned now from school shelves. There was also a collection of James Fennimore Cooper's Leatherstocking Tales; we were in former Iroquois territory so it was fun to read of their lives.

One day we came back to school after the summer recess to find a big KKK on the inside door. We could not understand its significance; even today I am not sure it was anything but a childish prank. We did have a black family living next to the school but they went to another school. There was even some antipathy to a Catholic family living in the area but we often played with George Soroka, son of Lithuanian emigrants.

The Eight Square School today

Smashed finger nail

After school one day us kids were walking home and passed an overhanging hickory nut tree; a nut was on the road, I rushed to pick it up while at the same time my buddy threw a rock intending to crack it open. The rock landed on my left hand middle finger smashing it and causing great pain. My father came to my rescue, he took me to the county fair then in progress and I temporarily forgot the pain. The nail never healed properly. When I was 84 years old I went to a podiatrist for a hammer toe; he could do nothing for the toe but prescribed terbenifine for a toe nail yeast infection to be taken daily over a three month period. Much to my amazement my misshapen 76 year old finger nail healed completely after the three months! Evidently all these years there had been a yeast infection under the nail that prevented it from returning to normal size and position.

First motion picture

School was a great experience for all us kids; it opened up the whole world to our insular existence. I remember one beloved teacher, Mrs. Carolyn Graves, who invited some of us kids to spend a night at her home in Dryden about 6 miles away just to let us see our first motion picture, a silent film about China in the High School auditorium. During the showing I proudly showed her how well I could read the captions. Incidentally this was also my introduction to a modern flush toilet! This teacher also was a cause for much grief; it was in 1936, she had just bought a new Ford V8 sedan and was using the wood shed some distance from the school as a garage during classes; I had carelessly left my sled in the path of her car when she ran over it backing up. I was devastated. But somehow I got another sled, perhaps from her or from an older sibling. One day in school Mrs. Graves, knowing how much we liked playing in the creek, took us there for a few hours of swimming. Later she somehow managed to remove her wet bra without removing her blouse, an interesting maneuver for us kids to watch! Another teacher, Francis Crane (later Mrs. Francis French), drove me back home after I came down with scarlet fever. I hated to miss school but had to stay away for a day or two, to prevent spread of the highly contagious disease.

Confirmation school

ummers were always anticipated with joy, even though I really enjoyed every day at school, for then we could go everywhere barefooted, it took a while though for our feet to get toughened up. One summer the mothers in the community decided that it was time for the older children to go to confirmation school, a requirement for all good Lutherans on reaching age thirteen. A preacher from Michigan gave us a week of instruction on the Bible in our school, at "graduation" the parents showed up for the ceremonies. Confirmation ended with an incredible performance by the wife of the pastor, she became filled with the spirit, going up and down the aisle screaming wildly, scaring us kids half to death! I could never decide whether it was part of the program or was a real religious experience for her.

Later an itinerant preacher, Mr. Tichenor (sp?), set up a Sunday school in a neighboring schoolhouse (probably sans permission though perfectly OK in the community of never-locked doors and no police presence). Several times I trudged the mile or so to the school for talks on biblical events. Our Finnish community at times invited a preacher from Michigan, likely an old acquaintance of a neighbor, to give a religious spiel and songfest party, a great event for the adults and the kids who listened to the adults sing at the top of their lungs in another room. After the singing, the parents gathered for coffee and home-baked cake; and the kids were invited. My mother reveled in these ceremonies, she greatly enjoyed the singing and conversation but my father would have nothing to do with anything religious.

Cow meets bull

It was about this time that I was asked by mother or father to lead a cow to one of our neighbors, I did not understand why this was needed but led the cow by a rope to our neighbors about ½ mile away. There the cow, in heat, was introduced to a bull. I still did not know what was going on and led the cow back home. We never were instructed on the "birds and bees".

Playing tricks on teacher

Another time our teacher was to take us for a walk to the nearby Fall Creek, a feeder to Cayuga Lake. It was near our school and was a favorite place for college students to come on a Saturday night to have a good time (it was appropriately called "Monkey Run"). We often went there on a Sunday morning to look for coins that fell from the revelers pockets during the trysts, we also found condoms. We had reconnoitered the spot before. We led the teacher to the spot by a path where we had placed a condom on a nearby branch from the previous students week-end party. We wanted to see what her reaction would be. She had no reaction and never suspected that it was a set-up.

Trapping animals

As boys had to resort to trapping animals to get any spending money (we never heard of allowances), One day I came to school after having caught and skinned a skunk; very little was said and the smell dissipated after a day or two. Actually a skunk pelt was only worth about a dime to the local fur peddler who drove by in his Ford Model A sedan to pick up animal pelts. I never could catch the more desirable red fox or mink but did get a weasel; this caused an emotional problem because before skinning it, I had to kill it; the only way I could do this was by drowning; the scream of the unfortunate creature remains imbedded in my mind to this day. Rabbits were often in the traps; their cry while twisting their head to break their neck was just as unsettling as that of the weasel. One time I caught a rabbit in the trap, the next day I had a full-blown case of impetigo, a bacterial skin disease caused usually by a streptococcus or staphylococcus; for a month I had to daub my face with an anti-bacterial salve; that was one time that the poor trapped creature had its revenge!

Games

In our one room school we had only one adult, the teacher, but the older children were frequently called upon to tell us what they had learned and it worked quite well. Discipline was no problem; the teacher was always believed to have a rubber hose handy although we never saw it used. We had signals for going to the outhouse (one finger, I believe) or for talking (two fingers?). During recess we played games; I recall "Annie, Annie, Over" where a ball is thrown over a building and every one switches sides; in the process the catcher tags someone who then goes to the tagger's side. "Red Light" was popular; the "It" counted to ten with eyes covered and everyone else tried to find a place to hide. Of course softball was popular with the boys but it was called "scrub" for lack of players enough for a regular team. The batter had to go to first base and back and avoid being tagged to score a point. In the winter, popular games were "King Of The Hill" and "Fox And Geese" providing there was sufficient snow. Of course we had snowball fights at every opportunity.

Father

My most memorable event from the early school days, though, was the time at recess playing in the road when a sheriff's car went by; in the back seat was my father on the way to jail probably for threatening mother. This was after the fire and life was tough. We had gone on relief; our parents had become violently antagonistic wrangling vociferously in Finnish and at great lengths at night over some incident at a neighbor's religious gathering, mother sitting on some mans lap, as far as we could determine. We kids were scared stiff, shivering in bed at night not knowing what the outcome of their arguments might be. I think this or some similar incident was the cause of my mother calling for the sheriff from a neighbors phone and sending him to jail in Ithaca. He was released shortly and came home in a suit given him by the sheriff. After that he would leave home for a week or more at a time with no explanation.

Dryden-Freeville Central School

After 6 years at the Eight Square Brick School I entered the Dryden-Freeville Central School having finished seventh grade; this was in 1939 when I was 12; I had skipped a grade (the third I believe).

For a country boy spending his first seven years at home and the next 5 years in a one room school, changing to a two story school for higher education was a quantum leap. Each class had its own classroom! The school had flush toilets! There were teachers for each class and the school was located in the thriving metropolis of Dryden (population of about 3000) with a hotel, grocery store, barber shop etc, etc.

A bus picked us up a half mile from our house but there was no communication network so we needed to use our own discretion during bad weather to decide whether or not to go to the bus stop a half mile away. I remember being snowed in for almost a week before a snow plow could clear our gravel road. We trudged through the snow to catch the bus. I learned that the words for the school anthem "Far Above The Towering Pine Trees" was written by the school custodian, Mr. Rockefeller, who lived on the school outskirts.

I do not know how large our class was in the beginning but we graduated with 32 students on June 25th, 1945. In addition to classes in English, History, Mathematics, French, Biology, etc. we had Gym where we practiced intramural basketball and engaged in athletic exercises; outdoors we played soccer or baseball. I was not great at sports but was awarded a big "D" number for playing soccer; in reality I think the only reason I made the team was because I was the only one available. I was manager of the school baseball team; my main duty consisted in putting the bases in place before each game. We were in a league with neighboring schools; I remember going to Homer, Marathon, and McGraw for soccer games. I do not remember ever winning a game. Our school could not afford to play football; indeed our soccer shoes were hand-me-downs; sometimes they were missing cleats.

We almost never missed going to school. Every day we walked the half mile to the bus stop for the yellow bus that was never late. Once though, my older brother persuaded me to play "hookey"; we played in a stream that day but kept an eye out for the truant officer ostensibly hired to round up miscreant students.

Farmers had difficulty getting help during the war, their sons were in Europe or the South Pacific; school kids were recruited, not unwillingly, to help farmers pick potatoes or harvest field corn for ensiling. We were the older students and were bused to the farmer's field for several hours of farm labor; we were paid, I recall, a dollar for our labors, a princely sum for poor country bumpkins in those days. I believe the federal government paid the farmers.

LC-USF33-021159-M5 Children gathering potatoes

Our war effort

We did have a good shop class; this was during WW II so in order to help the war effort we made wood replicas of enemy and our own planes for use by the armed forces for identification purposes. We had other wartime activities; because of the manpower shortage, we helped local farmers harvest potatoes or field corn and we were paid, I believe, $1 each time and were excused from classes. Another important war-connected activity for the Boy Scouts was collecting aluminum, an event organized by Dr. George H. Maughan. We went from house to house picking up un-needed aluminum pots and pans. Later I went to work for Dr. Maughan on his chicken farm.

Boy Scouts

At school I joined the local Boy Scout Troop; a signal event for this country lad; on the first camping trip it rained, and our pup tents leaked but what fun! We worked hard to advance to the next grade; at the time a 10 mile hike was a requirement for advancement to First Class. For Star or Eagle Scout a number of merit badges had to be earned. I made Senior Patrol Leader and Star Scout in the short time I was a scout. The scoutmaster was still active many years later.

First trip to dentist

In the town of Dryden there was a dentist, Dr. Ensign. I had never been to a dentist but during a physical examination the school doctor (Dr. Ryan was the school and town physician who had, I believe, a twin brother active in McLean) found considerable decay in my teeth. I had earned enough money helping local farmers to pay for the teeth repairs. A number of memorable long sessions of mechanical grinding by Dr. Ensign saved my teeth. He charged $14.50 for fixing 8 teeth. I still have all those teeth and owe Dr. Ensign a debt of gratitude. There was a barber in town, his name escapes me for now, who charged 25 cents for a haircut; but I do remember the brass spittoons in his shop!

Halloween

Halloween was the time for pranks; coming into town on the bus after Halloween we looked at a one horse wagon on top of the IGA store! Local pranksters had dismantled the wagon at night and re-assembled it there. In earlier years we kids had fun on Halloween by putting corn shocks on a road, or throwing rotten tomatoes at houses of people we did not like. I remember one case of tomato throwing where the owner started chasing us through the fields, I was the smallest and ran slowest so the owner caught me and gave me a tongue lashing but nothing else. In later years I was far more circumspect in my Halloween pranks; we never did any real harm though.

Stage plays

I was active in a stage production playing the leading role in "Dear Ruth". I also had a brief encounter with music in the form of a b-flat tuba. At the time I was also on the soccer team and after games, a special bus would bring us home but unfortunately in my case the bus driver dropped me off far from home so I had to carry the tuba 2 miles! I needed to practice during the week-end for a recital or something. I did not take the tuba home again and gave up trying to learn the instrument.

Working on farms

We made money by working for local farmers. I worked as a live-in hired hand at the Sykes farm in Etna from May to September 1942 at age 15. The farm had six cows, a pig and some chickens together with two horses, no tractor. Mr. Sykes assumed that I, coming from a farm background, would know how to milk cows but soon found out that it was not so. I quickly learned though after causing cases of an udder disease, garget, in improperly milked cows. The owner had severe asthma and during haying he had to often stop and use his inhaler. On Saturday mornings it was my job to churn the milk that had been souring for several days. The apparatus was a large wooden cylinder with a wooden paddle with a widened bottom. I had to lift the paddle up and down for several hours until the butter separated from the sour milk. On Saturdays we would go to Ithaca to sell the butter; then I would get paid my $3.50 for the week; some of it I spent on milk shakes, my first. I also bought my first camera with some of the money, it cost $1.35 and I carried it with me for the next 8 years, through college and the Marine Corps in WWII.

After the haying season in late summer, I was employed for $1/ day plus room and board by a larger dairy farm with 21 cows. I was such a proficient milker by this time that at the age 15, I could milk 11 cows to the owners 10. This nice owner, Mr. Harold Hanford, developed stomach cancer and died during the winter. Temporarily I had help from his son-in-law; later in the spring his son George left his freshman class at Cornell University in Ithaca to help at home. We ran the farm together for the summer of 1943. From October 1943 to July 1945 I worked in Etna earning $3.50/week plus room and board for

LC-USF33-T01-002639-M1

Dr. Maughan, a Mormon, a former chemistry teacher at the Cornell University Medical School in Ithaca that had been transferred to New York City. After the school transferred to NYC he stayed in Etna while his last child finished her studies at Cornell. He had gone into the egg business and built a 4 story chicken barn. I was the manager while he worked for GLF, a farm co-op in Ithaca, as a traveling farmer contact.

One of my duties was collecting and counting the eggs. I became so proficient at it that to this day I automatically keep count during routine activities, such as keeping track of reps in a gym. Once a week we would sort and candle the eggs with the help of a neighbor lady, Cary Lombard; this was done in the house cellar with a sorting machine, it was always amazing to find eggs that had two yolks. On Saturdays we would take the eggs to Ithaca and sell them at a large grocery store; they brought a premium price for their cleanliness and freshness.

Last years in High School

In 1944 I was a junior in the Dryden Central School and in Etna I was president of the "OK" club (Organization of Kids) in Houtz Hall. We were chaperoned by a few local adults. We had many good times there shooting baskets, dancing to 78 rpm records, or bidding on baskets of goodies that the girls brought; this was the way we got our dates for the evening! One evening we had a hay ride; I remember this very well because I lost my wallet containing $13! I looked high and low for it the next day but never found it.

Boys Town

In addition to being president of our junior class and senior patrol leader of the scout troop, I was sent to Manlius for a week of government studies in the Boys State program; this was made possible by the local American Legion who also had me recite Lincoln's Gettysburg Address at the Memorial Day service in the Dryden Square that year. But even at prestigious Boys State, where everyone had a "government" position, I was Water Commissioner, we could not resist being boys; one evening we lined up on the sides of a highway and leaned back pretending to have a rope stretched across the road; we howled when motorists slowed down or stopped!

Tragedy

The Maughans lived by Fall Creek, a tributary leading to Cayuga Lake, the second deepest of the Finger Lakes. One winter day we were alerted to noises from the opposite bank of the creek. The creek had frozen over but was not completely solid. A boy had tried to cross the creek and had fallen through the ice. Searchers tried to find the boy but he was never seen until the following spring when a neighbor's boy discovered the body on a sand bar a mile away.

Etna was a small village with one large building once used as a feed store for the local farmers. Later it was transformed into a small chemical factory producing soap for the farming community, the soap was advertised as being "Squeaky Clean". Etna also had a church, school, garage, general store and a post office as well as a bridge across the creek. The school was also one room but was of traditional wood construction. A railroad passed through the outskirts once or twice a day. My last grade school teacher, Francis Crane lived in Etna; during the war, my brother Evert had left his horse, Babe with her, for me to ride until he returned from the Army.

On to College

I was interested in pursuing a career in medicine (it turned out to be a pipe dream for a chicken farmer with no money!) and was approaching my 17th birthday; next year I would have to register for the draft. Dr. Maughan thought it would help my cause if I had some college experience before being drafted; I had just finished my junior year at Dryden but he succeeded in getting me into Cornell, 5 miles away, providing I could show passing grades in three required subjects: English, History and French. In August Dr. Maughan made arrangements with school officials for the three Dryden school teachers to give me special examinations on these subjects. After three months they gave me the special tests which I passed easily with good grades; Cornell accepted me for the winter term starting in late November.

Freshman year

ornell and most universities were on an accelerated schedule with two 6-months "years" each calendar year. I wore the traditional beanie for my freshman year that ended in late May 1946. Thus I finished my first year of college before I had officially graduated from high school! I was not legally graduated from Dryden High School until I passed the mandated New York State Regents exams! So I had to again cram like mad for less than a month after the Cornell "year" ended before taking the Regents exams with my class; I ended up with barely passing grades in English, History and French but could then claim my diploma from Dryden-Freeville Central School on graduation day. I have often wondered if those wonderful teachers had doctored the Regents test results in my favor!

I did have a difficult year at Cornell; I needed to hitch-hike five miles to Cornell, at times early on a Saturday morning. It was easy to get rides during the war and some Saturdays I could ride in with Dr. Hertel, the Secretary of the College of Agriculture who lived near the Maughans. Dr. Hertel was instrumental in enrolling me at the university. Hard times were to come. Chemistry was particularly difficult not having taken the High School course.

Drafted, chose Marines

month after the Regents exams I was drafted and chose the United States Marine Corps instead of the Army. With a year of ROTC at Cornell, I had been slated to join the Marines as an officer candidate, but in the interval before graduation, I developed appendicitis and the Marines no longer wanted me. When drafted in July, I chose the Marines and went off to Parris Island for boot training. During training for a Japan landing, the atom bomb was dropped; I was left in Hawaii, and after 9 months was relieved of further duty.

Microbiology Research

ubsequent to my studies at Dryden High School, I went on to graduate from Cornell with a major in Microbiology. Under the name C. N. Huhtanen I worked as a Research Microbiologist for 41 years with many peer reviewed research papers and a number of patents. Most species of animal life, including microbes, have scientific names derived from Latin. I always regretted not being able to take the mandated Latin class in my senior year. *quod est vita.*

Charles N. Huhtanen, Microbiologist

Epilogue

In this narrative I allude to reasons why my father was jailed; it definitely was not child abuse although he had chastised me on occasion with his fist; I was sassy and probably deserved the punishment. It was a lesson in behaving properly. Most families were nominally Lutheran and did not attend local churches; religious activity was limited to contacts with former Lutheran associates from Michigan. This was the reason for indoctrinating youngsters in their parent's previous faith with confirmation classes. College was not even dreamed of, all boys were expected to remain in a trade or become laborers, or stay in farming. Actually the reality of poor soil and even poorer soil drainage had penetrated the Finnish farming community and with the end of WWII other jobs became available. Farming was soon abandoned and assimilation with the greater community became irreversible. Without the intervention of Dr. Maughan it is unlikely that I would have received the encouragement to enter Cornell.

It should be noted that I do not have a PhD degree. After I graduated from Cornell with a BS I was invited to apply to a graduate program in the School of Agriculture but I declined as I had already been offered an intriguing microbiology research position. Later, the exigencies of a growing family made it even less desirable to pursue further education. I thoroughly enjoyed my 41 years in research; I was always allowed freedom to pursue research that would benefit my employer and only a very few peer reviewed papers were rejected by scientific journals.

Now, whenever I feel ignorant, I turn to my infallible mentor, Wikipedia; it admirably fulfills my needs. The following publications were retrieved from a search through Google.

Acknowledgments

It is only right to thank the teachers, most probably long since passed away, for their efforts far above their mandated tutorial obligations, for opening, and holding open, the door to opportunity.

Thanks to Dr George H. Maughan, long since deceased, who was instrumental in providing entry to Cornell University at a critical juncture of my life.

Thanks to my daughter, Shirley Huhtanen, President of Renaissance Data Systems Inc. who so carefully scrutinized and emended the manuscript before sending it on to the publisher, Trafford Press.

Thanks to the Library of Congress for maintaining and providing access to pictures of life during the Great Depression for the Farm Security Administration/ Office of War Information.

Eight Square School, 1936: The Huhtanen Children; a
Charles; b George (Evert);c Aina; d Esther

Charles Huhtanen, Port Richey, Florida 2006

C. N. Huhtanen Publications

1. Effect of Ultrasound on Disaggregation of Milk Bacteria. C.N. Huhtanen. J. Dairy Sci.49:1008-1010.
2. Nitrosamines and the Inhibition of Clostridia in Medium Heated with Sodium Nitrite. A.E. Wasserman and C.N. Huhtanen. J. Food Sci. 37:785. 1972.
3. Effect of Acids on Selenite Inhibition of *Salmonella typhimurium* and *Salmonella dublin*. C. N. Huhtanen. J. Food Prot. 41:289-290. 1978.
4. Inhibition of *Clostridium botulinum* by Aliphatic Amines and Long Chain Aliphatic Aminodiamides. C.N. Huhtanen and T.J. Micich. J. Amer. Oil Chem. Sci. 55:854. 1979.
5. Inhibition of *Clostridium botulinum* by P-Hydroxybenzoic Acid N-Alkyl Esters. M. Dymicky and C.N. Huhtanen. Anti. Micr. Agents Chemother. 6: 298-301. 1979.
6. Inhibition of *Clostridium botulinum* by Spice Extracts and Aliphatic Alcohols. C.N. Huhtanen. Appl. Environ. Micr. 39:818-822. 1980.
7. Incidence and Origin of *Clostridium botulinum* Spores in Honey. C.N. Huhtanen, D. Knox and H. Shimanuki. J. Fd. Prot. 44:812-814. 1981.
8. Antibotulinal Activity of Methyl and Ethyl Fumarates in Comminuted Nitrite-Free Bacon. C.N. Huhtanen and E.J. Guy. J. Food Sci. 48:1574.1983.
9. A Research Note: Antifungal Properties of Esters of Alkenoic and Alkynoic Acids. C.N. Huhtanen and E.J. Guy. J. Food Sci. 49: 1954.
10. Nitrite Substitutes for Controlling *Clostridium botulinum*. C.N. Huhtanen. Devel. Ind. Micro. 1984.
11. Use of Irradiation to Ensure the Microbiological Safety of Processed Meats. D.W. Thayer, R.V. Lachica, C.N. Huhtanen and E. Wierbicki. Food Technol. 40:159. 1986.
12. Gamma Radiation Sensitivity of *Listeria monocytogenes*. C.N. Huhtanen, R.K. Jenkins and D.W. Thayer. J. Food Prot. 52:610-613. 1989.
13. Gamma Radiation Inactivation of Enterococci. C.N. Huhtanen. J. Food Prot. 53:302-305. 1990.
14. Inhibition of *Clostridium botulinum* Toxin Formation by C.*sporogenes* in Media and in a Meat System. C.N. Huhtanen. J. Food Prot. 54, 1991.
15. Gamma Radiation Resistance of *Clostridium botulinum* 62A and *Bacillus subtilis* Spores in Honey. C.N. Huhtanen. J. Food Prot. 54. 1991.
16. The effect of calcium salts on chlortetracycline absorption. E.L.R. Stokstad, J.M.Pensack, C.N.Huhtanen. Antib. Annual, 70, 879-83 1959.
17. Manometric estimation of rumen urease. C.N.Huhtanen and L.S.Gall. J. Bact. 69(1) 102-3. 1955.
18. CO2 utilization by rumen microorganisms. C.N.Huhtanen, F J.Carleton and H.R Roberts. J. Bact. 68(6) 749-51. 1954.
19. Inhibition of *Clostridium botulinum* by 5-nitrothiazole. M.Dymicky, C.N.Huhtanen and A.E.Wasserman. Antimicr. Agents Chemo. 12(3): 353.1977.

www.ingramcontent.com/pod-product-compliance
Lightning Source LLC
Chambersburg PA
CBHW061226280526
45784CB00006B/2651